Let's Be Honest

LET'S BE HONEST

REAL ANSWERS FOR REAL
WOMEN FACING ABUSE

Krystle Laughter

Let's Be Honest: *Real Answers for Real Women Facing Abuse*

© 2020 by Krystle Laughter

Published by Fortre Publishing Co.
Tacoma, WA 98409

Printed in the United States of America

All right reserved. No part of this publication may be reproduced, stored in a retrieval system, or transmitted in any form or by any means-electronic, digital, photocopy, recording, or any other- except for brief quotations in printed reviews, without the prior written permission of the author.

All Scripture quotations, unless otherwise stated, are taken from the New Living Translation. Holy Bible, New Living Translation, copyright © 1996, 2004, 2015 by Tyndale House Foundation. Used by permission of Tyndale House Publishers, Inc., Carol Stream, Illinois 60188. All rights reserved.

Scripture quotations marked NIV have been taken from the New International Version®, Holy Bible, New International Version®, NIV® Copyright © 1973, 1978, 1984, 2011 by Biblica, Inc.® Used by permission. All rights reserved worldwide.

Cover & Interior Design by Krystle Laughter

I S B N 978-1-7346951-2-0

TABLE OF CONTENTS

Introduction

Let's Be Honest: A Poem

Section 1:
About Abuse

-How Do You Break the Cycle of Abuse?

-Why Do You Think It's so Hard to Speak Up and Talk About the Things That Are Happening to You?

-How Do I Cope with the Trauma from Abuse?

-How Did You Feel About Exposing Your Abuser?

-Does Your Abuser Act Like Nothing Happened After He Hits You?

-How Many Abusive Relationships Have You Been In?

-What Red Flags Did You Ignore?

TABLE OF CONTENTS

Section 2:
Is This Abuse?

-Is Being Jealous, Clingy, and Accusing me of Cheating Abuse?

-Is a Person Toxic Because They Try to Control Who You Associate with and Be Around?

-Is Intimidation Considered Abuse?

-Is a Partner Always Blaming Me for Things Abuse?

-What Are the Signs of Emotional Abuse?

Why Me?

Section 3:
Abuse with Children

-Should I Stay for the Kids?

-Do You Ever Wonder How Abuse Affects Your Kids?

TABLE OF CONTENTS

-Has Anyone Been Able to Keep Their Kids Away from Their Abuser?

-I Can't Afford to Take Care of the Kids by Myself. What Should I Do?

-I'm Pregnant with My Abuser's Child. How do I Start Over When I Feel Stuck?

-Has Anyone Else's Child Taken the Side of the Abuser?

Section 4:
Staying with an Abuser

-Why Does My Abuser Always Make Me Feel Like I'm the Problem?

-Can an Abusive Man Change?

-Why Am I the Only Woman He's Ever Hit?

Is It Normal to Feel Like I Don't Know Who I am Anymore?

TABLE OF CONTENTS

Is Staying Worth It?

Section 5:
Leaving an Abuser

-How Did You Find the Strength to Leave?

-How Did You Stop Yourself from Going Back to Your Abuser After You Left?

-When Do the Nightmares Stop?

-How Did You Stop Missing Him?

-How Many Times Did It Take You to Leave for Good?

-Has Anyone's Abuser Gone to Jail, Gotten Help & Stopped Being Abusive Towards You?

-What Was Your Experience When You Went to Court to Get a Protection Order?

TABLE OF CONTENTS

-How Do You End It?

-How Long Does it Take to Heal Before Trying to Find Love Again?

Why Do I Miss My Abuser?

Section 6:
Women of Faith Facing Abuse

-Is Abuse God's Way of Punishing Me?

-Did Your Abuser Ever Use Your Faith Against You?

-Was Anyone Else Mad at God for the Abuse?

-My Abuser Says He's a Christian

-Can I Divorce My Abuser?

About the Author

Books

The answer to every question you have is already on the inside of you. You just have to learn how to trust yourself again.

Let's Be Honest

(a poem)

Let's be honest,

Spread a little hope

Let's tell the truth

Give them strength to cope.

Let's be honest

To the victims trying to survive

Who have no place to go,

No place to run and hide.

Let's be honest

To those with no words left to say,

The desperate and confused

Those who've lost their way.

Let's be honest,

Show them how we got through.

Let's be honest

With those who don't know what to do.

Let's be honest

To those tired of being strong.

Let's just be honest with them,

And show them they're not alone.

INTRODUCTION

Domestic violence is a terrifying and confusing thing to experience. As a survivor, I understand the inner turmoil and emotions you're experiencing as you try to get back to a normal life. This book is not the 'end all be all book' on domestic violence. It's simply a glimpse into the plight of women like you, who are trying to make sense of being abused. Should I stay? Should I go? Is this abuse? The questions we carry as victims of domestic violence can overwhelm us and make us feel stuck, and having children and a lack of resources further complicate these questions.

This book aims to provide answers and hope for women in abusive relationships. My goal is to help you find your way out of domestic violence by giving you insight and understanding into your own experiences through the lens of other survivors. You are not alone. I, and the many women who have been there, stand with you, hand in hand, and we're rooting for you. You can be free. You can break the cycle of abuse. Domestic violence doesn't have to be your eternal fate. I believe in you, and I can't wait to see you on the other side of this.

-xoxo

Section 1:
About Abuse

"Someone once asked me how I hold my head up so high after all I have been through. I said it's because no matter what, I am a survivor, not a victim."

- Patricia Buckley

Question:

How do I break the cycle of abuse?

Answers:

Refuse to be a part of it, build a support system, and put distance between you and that person.
-K.

Run and don't look back. Leave everything. You can always get more stuff. Start talking to a DV counselor.
-C.

There's no one size fits all answer. It took me years of counseling, discovering myself, and building a support system. I was still with him while I was doing all of these and I felt helpless to leave, but one day he raped me and I decided it was going to be the last time. That gave me the final push I needed to leave him, but I couldn't have done it without the other things I worked hard at.
-T.

Years and years of therapy for myself. I realized that I didn't have the power to change him.
-A.

It may be hard to hear, but at the end of the day staying in an abusive relationship is a choice.

-S.

Education is the key. We need to understand all the different faces of domestic violence. Secondly, we need to educate our youth so that we can break the cycle.

-A.

Having boundaries. No is a complete sentence.

-C.

Leaving your abuser, so that the children don't learn his ways. Teach them right from wrong.

-P.

I decided that I was no longer going to be a victim. Readjust your crown and realize you are victorious. You got this!

-A.

Stop dating a-- holes. It boils down to you really. You get to choose.

-E.

Question:

Why do you think it's so hard to speak up and talk about the things that are happening to you?

Answers:

I initially felt afraid of being judged. I got so used to holding everything together that I didn't know how to open up to people I knew I could trust. It takes time. There are still some things I've only told a few people, because I feel ashamed, but I think that's okay.

-K.

Feeling judged, finger pointing, blame game, not feeling listened to, not feeling like I have a voice, and the biggest... not being believed.

-V.

I kept it a secret for ten years. I finally told a friend after being asked directly about it. I'm not a good liar. That was a turning point, but it took me many years later to actually leave.

-P.

For me, I always told myself that I would never be in this kind of situation, so when I was, it was embarrassing. Even though I knew it wasn't my fault, I still felt guilty for not seeing the red flags.

-V.

For me it was the thought of being judged or embarrassed.

-A.

I felt like no one would believe me. I thought because he never put me in the hospital it wasn't really that bad.

-T.

The victim blaming and shaming involved.

-A.

It was a nightmare I don't ever want to remember, that's why I didn't tell anyone else.

-I.

I was ashamed until I realized just how many other women are going through the same thing. If telling my story could help another person feel like she's not alone, or help someone leave an abusive situation, then it's worth it.

-L.

Question:

How do I cope with the trauma from abuse?

Answers:

Therapy is what ultimately helped me to get my life back. Also, just stay busy. I'll try to do a relaxing activity, coloring, reading a book, watching silly videos online, etc.
-B.

I found that reading books has helped me. I found some good series online.
-B.

Get therapy. Discover who you are, what you like. Find out what you want in life and do it. Once you're free, you realize that you are free to live your life however you want. Whatever you choose, make it something you can be proud of.
-L.

In therapy I learned how to breathe and talk myself through it. I also read a lot, take short walks, and pray. This by far has been the most difficult thing to deal with.
-T.

My friends helped me out a lot.
-O.

Don't try to do it yourself. You need the support. I know it can be hard, but find a support system; join a group, go to counseling, and find trustworthy friends who encourage you.
-K.

Find a safe place to talk about your pain. If you don't release your pain it will build up and manifest itself through anxiety. It will be hard at first but you can do it.
-T.

I listen to music, go walking, talk to friends, and spend time with my kids.
-R.

Disrupting the negative thoughts with exercise, prayer, and calling a girlfriend. I also take medication.
-C.

Always, always have a counselor. Write down your goals and go back to them when you can't think straight. Most importantly, breathe. Breathe through every thought. Keep positive thoughts. Focusing on these things helps keep me positive.
-D.

Therapy, prayer, running, walking, writing, and a punching bag (seriously). I Avoid triggers if possible. I have a great support group with my therapist.

-F.

For me finding a creative outlet like poetry, journaling, singing, and drawing really helped me.

-W.

Therapy, support groups, and education. I started reading books about domestic violence to get new knowledge. It has really helped.

-C.

A lot of self-care. Go get your nails done or have a spa day at home. Be patient with yourself, buy yourself something small or take yourself out on a date. Love yourself the way you wish others would.

-K.

For me it was taking one day at a time, and listening to a lot of inspirational music, and book reading.

-W.

Question:

How did you feel about exposing your abuser?

Answers:

I once heard someone say, if a person didn't want to be exposed for doing something wrong, then they should've thought about that before they did it. I think that's a great way to think about it. You don't owe it to your abuser to keep his dirty little secret. You owe it to yourself to live a life that is full and free, and that involves telling the truth about what happened to you. You have no reason to feel guilty or ashamed.

-K.

I didn't feel ashamed about outing him. I felt bad for putting up with it for as long as I did.

-A.

Initially I felt hesitant because I was worried what others would think about me. Isn't that something? I was the one worried when he's the one who did the wrong thing. I have since learned that I have no reason to feel ashamed for my experience. It was a painful life lesson, but I've learned a lot from it, and now I'm helping other women.

-D.

I think it depends on the severity of the abuse you suffered. For some victims it may not be a wise choice to out their abuser publicly. I think everyone needs to do what's best for them.

-O.

I say do what's good for you. Only you can determine that. If you feel like others need to know because he has everyone deceived, then that's up to you. Just know that not everyone will want to believe you, even with evidence.

-L.

My abuser was arrested and his cousin found out about it. I heard through word of mouth that he was mad at me. I thought that was ridiculous. Just goes to show how some people will never support you, but that's okay. I know I didn't do anything wrong.

-D.

I didn't want to out my abuser because we have children together. If they find out on their own, then that's that. I feel no need to expose anyone. I believe every person will get what they have coming to them, and he will eventually expose himself.

-A.

Nope. Put your energy into yourself, not at getting back at him or putting him out there. He will do that all on his own.

-T.

Question:

Does your abuser act like nothing happened after he hits you?

Answers:

Yes. He would act like everything was normal and if I brought it up he would tell me that I had to forgive him because I'm a Christian.

-K.

Yup. Years later he still acts like nothing ever happened.

-J.

Yes. I think it's a mind game thing. If he can make you question yourself and make you feel like you're going crazy, he's won. It's really inhumane.

-K.

Yes. I think some abusers are so far gone that they actually believe they didn't do anything wrong.

-O.

Yep. He beat me. I was swollen with a fat lip, swollen eye, and he even tried to have sex with me and wanted to cuddle afterwards. He kept telling me to stop pouting.

-W.

Every time. Now I have a different life and spend time doing a lot of self care and getting past triggers and PTSD.

-J.

Yes, and it annoyed me so bad. He punched me in the face, broke my jaw. He even came to the hospital with me. Every time I mentioned him breaking my jaw he would act like he didn't know what I was talking about. He would deny ever doing it.

-G.

Yes, my ex abuser did this all the time.

-H.

The next day it's like nothing happened. They are monsters.

-M.

Every time. He would say that I had to do better or that I was crazy and that it didn't happen. He made me think that I was the crazy one.

-L.

Mine did. He would never apologize.

-K.

Question:

How many abusive relationships have you been in?

Answers:

From childhood, both fathers of my three daughters, and both of my husbands. My last relationship was severe psychological, financial, and emotional abuse.
-M.

Two. The first was fifteen years long with two kids. The second one was twenty-four years and one kid. Don't know which one was worse. Anyway, both of them were bad.
-K.

Both marriages. The first one I had two kids. It was physically, emotionally, and financially abusive. The second one was five children and it was mental and emotional abuse. I didn't realize it was abuse until the end.
-J.

Three. First one eighteen years, second two years, and the last one was eight years long.
-M.

All four of my serious relationships were somewhat abusive, until I got to my fifth and we had a baby. I guess I got lucky with him.

-S.

Three. My first boyfriend of two and a half years, my second marriage of twenty-two years, then a partner after him was another two and a half years. Now I know the red flags and have an amazing man.

-C.

Just one. He choked me in the kitchen at a party. He was drunk. At that moment I knew I would leave him although it took me a couple of weeks. I packed my things and left. I blocked him, that was three years ago.

-S.

My father was an emotionally abusive and distant alcoholic father. I've always gone for the same type of man. My past boyfriends never physically abused me, but I ended up married to one for thirteen years. I guess we go for what we know.

-W.

Several. My father was abusive too. My grandma removed me from the house when I was a teenager, because he was on the verge of punching me in the face. It really messes up our lives.

-T.

My childhood was abusive. I then vowed to never be in that type of relationship, but I ended up married to a man who didn't hit me until after we were married.

-M.

Two abusive marriages. The first was an amateur, the second was a professional.

-Q.

One. I was with him for almost four years. I'm thankful that was my only experience with an abusive partner. My current boyfriend is awesome. He treats me very well.

-G.

Two, if you exclude my childhood.

-W.

Question:

What red flags did you ignore?

Answers:

He was very isolated. He didn't have any friends. I think that's often overlooked. He also thought he was better than everybody else and always criticized others.

-K.

Their past relationships. Do they always blame their "crazy" ex? There are two sides to every story.

-I.

His anger problems when he didn't get his way.

-F.

He was always the victim. Nothing was ever his fault.

-G.

On our first meeting he told me that God said I was his wife. I didn't realize just how weird and fanatical that is until now. Scary when I think about it. He didn't even know me or how old I was. When I told my age he breathed a sigh of relief.

-C.

His age. He was much older than me. It is important to understand that older partners have more life experience and can use that to their advantage to abuse you and make you feel less than.

-A.

He always had something to say. My clothing was too tight or I was too sarcastic. He never had good things to say about me. It was like his goal was to break me down from the beginning.

-J.

Inconsistency, blaming others, easily angered, I could go on and on.

-L.

He always had to be the center of attention, like he had to prove something. He was very insecure and made everything about him.

-Y.

A close relative of mine passed away. He started sulking and had no comforting words for me. When I asked him what was wrong he stated that he felt he was to blame for the death. He didn't even know the relative. He had a disturbing way of making everything all about him.

-I.

He would abuse and torture my kitten.

-T.

He had severe mood swings and depression. I thought I could save him and bring joy to his life. Boy was I wrong. Some people enjoy being miserable. When I was the most miserable I'm pretty sure I could see a slight smirk on his face, like he had accomplished his goals. Sick!

-N.

He would criticize me and get angry with me for silly things. He made me feel like I was going crazy.

-C.

He would call me prideful and arrogant because I wasn't attracted to him. He was older, balding, and overweight. He broke me down until I finally caved in. I should've never settled. One of the biggest regrets of my life. He turned out to be a monster.

-I.

Section 2:
Is This Abuse?

"Don't let someone who doesn't know your value tell you how much you're worth."

- Unknown

Question:

Is jealousy, being clingy, and accusing me of cheating abuse?

Answers:

It's a sign of him being super insecure which is a red flag and something I wouldn't put up with as a grown woman. Let him go!
-A.

Yes. Red flags I wish I saw sooner.
-E.

Absolutely. It's a form of control. They think you're their property.
-P.

They usually accuse you of doing what they are doing.
-C.

My ex accused me of cheating all the time while I was at work. He eventually went on to say the baby I was carrying wasn't his' either. Don't fall for it. It's all a game to keep you emotionally distraught and constantly seeking his approval. Run!
-N.

Yes. He's always looking over my shoulder to who I'm talking to over the phone.
-A.

That led up to my ex putting a loaded gun to my head and threatening to kill me.
-M.

My ex used to accuse me of cheating during my bathroom breaks when I was in school full time. The accusations they make are ridiculous and you shouldn't take it to heart. They are unstable and irrational people. Move on. No one deserves to be treated that way.
-K.

Guilty conscious, blaming you for doing what he's doing.
-A.

Yep. I just broke up with a guy I was dating for six months because of this. He always acted suspicious and paranoid.
-K.

If anything, those are super red flags because it shows that they can't control their emotions, which can lead to abuse.
-S.

Question:

Is a person toxic because they try and control who you associate with and be around?

Answers:

Yes, it's toxic and no you shouldn't have to keep on reassuring them and trying to prove things to them. The only thing that can fix an insecure person is the person himself.

-M.

Yes. Jealousy breeds abuse. Him not trusting you is a red flag and indicative of isolation.

-C.

If I would've stood my ground on that red flag and not made excuses for him, I would have not had to call the cops over eleven times in less than a month, almost lost my job and my home all because he's trying to kill me. Trust your gut. If it feels off, leave. I wish I did. I would've saved myself years of pain.

-T.

Big red flag! I wish I had paid attention to it. I stayed for twelve years. I ended up being isolated from everyone. It was exhausting. I even lost my female friends because he always thought they were trying to hook me up with someone else. Run!

-A.

If you have to ask if it's toxic, then you already know the answer.

-O.

Absolutely. You are not a child. You have the right to be around whoever you want. No one has the right to control that, even if your partner doesn't like the person.

-I.

Question:

Is intimidation considered abuse?

Answers:

Yes. I wish I had understood this before. I only got worse.
-O.

Absolutely. My abuser would give me a certain look and it was the most threatening look ever. No man should look at women the way he would look at me. It's like he had hatred in his eyes.
-K.

It is. It's mental and emotional abuse, because sometimes the threat of danger is worse than the actual experience. It's very scary.
-A.

My ex used to charge at me like he was going to hurt me. It's like he liked knowing I was afraid.
-L.

Yes. I'm happy I left that toxic relationship. I feel so much lighter. I finally feel worthy of the love I know I deserve.
-H.

Yes, for sure. My scars have healed, but the actions hurt me mentally. I just don't get how he can say I love you. In the end, actions speak louder than words.
-A.

He told me he was proud of himself for punching a hole in the wall instead of me.
-L.

To me it's the worst kind, the thought of walking on eggshells, because you don't know when it will happen. That's the worst.
-M.

Yes it is. They know what they're doing. They get satisfaction knowing that you're scared. It disgusts me when I think about it. Real men don't abuse women. I know that now.
-S.

Yes. My husband loves to use various intimidation tactics.
-M.

Question:

Is my partner always blaming me for things abuse?

Answer:

Blaming is a form of emotional abuse. Blame happens when a partner refuses to take responsibility for his actions, usually by shifting blame to the other partner. Blame-shifting is a devastating form of abuse because the victim suffers mental and emotional distress and confusion and begins to question his sanity. Additionally, the refusal of the blaming partner to accept responsibility for his actions in the relationship causes further emotional trauma to the victimized partner.

As a result, the victimized partner then begins to walk on eggshells believing they are the source of the problems in the relationship. In a feeble attempt to keep the peace, the victimized partner tries to comply with her partner's demands. This strategy is useless because the real issue lies with the blame-shifting partner. Thus a never-ending cycle of abuse ensues.

It's hard when someone refuses to take responsibility for his actions. The pain we feel when we are wrongly blamed for things is heartbreaking. In my experience with a blame-shifting partner, I found it impossible to reason and be logical with him.

It seems as though his heart was set on only wanting to see his side of the story. My countless attempts to show both sides of the issue and create a space where everyone felt heard were useless because my partner didn't want to see how his actions hurt and affected others.

Please understand that blaming is not a healthy or normal form of communication within a relationship. If your partner is using blame to avoid the consequences of his behavior, be aware and get out. In healthy relationships, two people communicate their feelings and concerns with one another to resolve issues and future conflicts.

In an abusive relationship, the abuser aims to keep you in a confused and emotionally dependent state to maintain power and control over you. Love cannot blossom in this type of environment. Love is an action word. If someone's actions consistently don't align with his words, he doesn't honestly care for you. There is someone out there who will love and honor you. Move on and refuse to accept less than you deserve.

-K.

Question:

What are the signs of emotional abuse?

Answer:

Emotional abuse is not as obvious as some other forms of abuse like physical abuse. Although the evidence isn't as easily seen, the effects of emotional abuse can last longer than the scars of physical violence. Below is a list of signs of emotional abuse.

-You have to get permission to socialize with your friends and family.

-Your partner destroys your personal belongings

-You are often accused of cheating with little to no evidence.

-Your partner undermines and/or ignores your feelings

-You walk on eggshells and are afraid to mention certain topics with your partner.

-Your partner humiliates you in public and in private.

-Your partner threatens to harm themselves, you, and/or your children if you ever leave them.

-Your partner harms or threatens to harm your pets.

-Your partner sabotages your efforts to be involved in social events. For example, he tells your secrets, tries to embarrass you, belittle you, etc.

-Your partner's behavior is unpredictable. You never know what mood they will be in.

-Your partner gives you the silent treatment when you want to talk about things.

-Your partner is resentful of children's needs.

-Your partner sabotages your schedule and outside commitments.

-Has no sympathy for others wants, needs, feelings, or concerns.

Question:

Why Me?

Answer:

If you've ever asked yourself this question, you're not alone. I have laid awake many nights asking myself why abuse had to happen to me. I've tried to figure out what it was about me that attracted me to him. Was I insecure? Did I give off a certain vibe? The truth is that I still don't have the answer to this question, and I probably never will. It's human nature to want to understand things because we can do something about it once we understand something. Not knowing why the abuse happened can make victims feel vulnerable and like they have to live in fear of it happening again.

Like me, you may never know why your abuser chose you, but you can still be proactive and find healing. I want to challenge you to shift your focus off 'why me' because that line of thinking will keep you stuck. Instead, I want you to think about what you can do now so that abuse never happens to you again. You can do this by getting information and knowledge about abuse, learning about red flags, building your self-confidence, and creating a support system. The more you know, the more you'll grow and be less likely to fall into an abusive relationship.

Reflecting on my abusive relationships, I discovered I was vulnerable because I witnessed abuse as a child. I was also never taught about self-love, mutual respect, and boundaries within an intimate relationship, so when I saw red flags, I didn't see them for the deal-breaker they were. I just hoped and prayed that things would get better.

I accepted abuse not because I believed I deserved it. I didn't know how to get out once I realized I was in an abusive relationship. It would be best if you, too, learned the art of self-reflection. Did you witness abuse growing up? Were you abused growing up? Did you see healthy female and male role models? Were you taught about self-love? If not, it's no wonder you were vulnerable to abuse. What you have to understand is that abuse is not your fault. You could be the most confident, beautiful, successful woman, and abuse could still happen to you. Many women are caught off guard because abusers are good at hiding who they really are.

The good news is that abuse didn't happen to you because something is wrong with you. Let me assure you that no matter what you've been told. You don't deserve bad treatment. You deserve someone who will love, honor, respect, and protect you. You are enough! Healing begins when you begin to understand that nothing you do, say, or experience can decrease your worthiness as a human being. Say this with me until you believe it.

I am loved.

I am worthy of love.

I don't deserve abuse.

Abuse is not my fault.

Abuse isn't my future.

I am not a victim.

I am victorious.

I am powerful.

I am strong.

I am learning.

I am growing.

My future is bright.

Section 3:
Abuse with Children

"When it comes to abuse, you believe there's no way out. There is always help. There is always a way out."

- Rev. Donna Mulvey

Question:

Should I stay for the kids?

Answers:

God no! Don't stay for them; leave for them and show them they deserve better.
-H.

Show them that they don't have to tolerate someone's abusive behavior by leaving.
-G.

I tried to stay for the kids. My kiddos are very young, all five and under. He started abusing the kids too. I left with no money and no support from anyone. It's the best thing I could've done for them.
-C.

No. Children learn how to be abusive from their parents.
-I.

Hell no! Get out. The kids don't need to grow up seeing you be abused.
-G.

No, it's not worth it. I almost lost my life.
-T.

I used to think the same thing, but I realized that the more they're around him the more likely that they'll turn out to be like him. I left.

-P.

You have to ask yourself, Is this the kind of home that I want my children to grow up in? Put yourself in their shoes. They depend on you to keep them safe. Is your home safe?

-A.

I did. The worst mistake I've ever made. Please leave.

-B.

No. Never stay for the kids. It's more damaging to them than beneficial. You can provide a better environment for them.

-T.

Leave for the kids. It is better for them to see you alone and happy than miserable and abused.

-R.

I did for a while, but I finally got out.

-K.

My mom left for us and I couldn't be more grateful to her.

-F.

I tried staying and it's not worth the heartache of watching your kids suffer daily. The children end up with much more trauma. Leave for the kids. You won't regret it. You will regret staying though.

-B.

You don't want to raise kids who think abuse is the way to solve your problems.

-M.

No, especially not for the kids. If kids are involved, that should be the reason to leave. If not for yourself, do it for them, because he will start doing to them what he did to you.

-J.

The kids will be happier. They are watching and learning even when you don't think they are.

-T.

Leave for the kids. Don't let him get a chance to use them against you. If he loved you he wouldn't hurt their mother.

-R.

Call the DV hotline in your state. They have lots of resources to help you. Staying is just not worth it.

-P.

Children grow up and leave home. If you stay, you will lose yourself. Show your kids how strong you are and leave. Your strength will give them courage.

-G.

If you stay they'll have to deal with things like anxiety, lack of confidence, and more. I thought I couldn't do it until I realized that I already was.

-Y.

I didn't stay because of my kid.

-W.

Question:

Do you ever wonder how abuse affects your kids?

Answers:

I don't have to wonder. They went through a lot of therapy. It was a lot.//
-M.

My son has nightmares.//
-A.

I went through it with multiple of my mother's relationships. I ended up in a DV relationship myself and I suffer from depression. It has a big impact on kids.//
-M.

My son has really bad anxiety. He didn't like leaving me alone for a while.//
-R.

My oldest daughter has severe mood swings and PTSD from the abuse. My middle has severe anxiety, depression, and suicidal tendencies.//
-M.

A lot. My three sons are still in counseling and I left my abuser nine years ago.

-G.

My oldest is five. He still freaks out at the sound of loud noises. If anyone moves fast towards him he flinches.

-L.

I grew up in a chaotic home. My dad was abusive and I was his punching bag. I was diagnosed with anxiety, PTSD, and trauma. I'm still trying to get over it at the age of twenty-three.

-S.

Two of my kids blame me, not realizing I saved them by leaving their dad. It is what it is I guess.

-I.

Yes. My daughter witnessed so much. I hope now that I'm free she can put it out of her mind.

-A.

I am fifty years old and I grew up in an abusive household and it still affects me until this day. It never goes away. Take your children and run. Because of the abuse I experienced growing up I made the decision to never have kids.

-P.

Question:

Has anyone been able to keep their kids away from their abuser? We have an order of protection against him. I don't want him getting in their heads and messing them up.

Answers:

Yes, it's possible. If you have any recordings or anything, keep them and use them in court. You need evidence.
-B.

Unless you have concrete proof he's a danger to your children, it is extremely hard.
I fought for three years and my daughter sent me a picture of his ID next to a line of cocaine, and that's finally what sealed the deal. She had been saying she was scared of him for a long time before that and the courts did nothing.
-N.

If you have the children on the protection order, then that should cover you.
-I.

Yes. I initially had to do supervised visits even after he tried to kill me. It was my word against his'. His mother did the visits at her house, but after she passed away there was no one else to do the visits. I haven't seen him since. I was sad initially, but he used her to continue abusing me.
Karma is real.
-K.

It's super hard, but not impossible. Gather any and all evidence. Once your protection order expires, you will need new evidence to extend or renew it.
-V.

Yes! I went to court and got sole custody, and visitation only if the kids want to see him, which they don't.
-J.

Yes, it's possible. All of my three kids have autism and I was able to get full custody of them, and moved to another state away from my kids' father.
-M.

In my experience, my abuser didn't want to be an active father once we were no longer together. He has never paid his child support, but I don't care. I'm just glad to have him out of our lives.
-K.

You can get supervised visits. That will discourage him from wanting to see them, eventually he will fall off and then you can get his visits suspended. Do whatever you need to protect your children.
-P.

Yep. I have a five year restraining order against him.
-L.

I was told I had to let him see them because he never abused them, only me.
-S.

Question:

I can't afford to take care of my kids by myself. What should I do?

Answers:

There are many resources out there to help people in your situation. You have options.

-P.

Abusers can make you believe that you can't make it without their help. What you have to realize is that you made it before them and you'll make it after them.

-M.

I know the feeling, but you have to start believing in yourself. You can do it. There are people and organizations that will help you.

-B.

I think it's a mental thing. Abuse breaks you down to the point where you don't believe you're capable of doing things on your own anymore. Remember who you were before abuse. You have the power to change and create the life you want for your children. Don't let anyone else convince you otherwise, not even yourself.

-T.

I know it's scary, but you can do this. Imagine the life you want for yourself, baby, and let that be your motivation.

-A.

Don't give up. Nowadays, there are stay-at-home jobs you can do over the phone. You might qualify for free childcare from the state, you can get food stamps to buy food, and if you qualify, the state will pay for medical care for you and your children. You have more options than you realize.

-S.

Save up if you can. Make a plan of how much money you need to start over and hide it in a safe place. Create a safety plan, get out, and put your abuser on child support if it's safe to do so. You can do this. It just may take some time.

-T.

You may have to take a leap of faith. If you don't have the money, you can find a shelter, they will supply you with resources and connect you to the right places and people. The alternative is staying, continuing to be abused, and living hell on earth. Leaving can seem scary, but staying isn't any better either. You just have to make a choice.

-M.

You have to start believing in yourself. You can take care of your kids. There are resources and places that will help you.

-P.

There's help out there. Call your local shelters, find a support group if it's safe, and save money if you can, even if it's only a little bit at a time.

-Y.

Question:

I'm pregnant with my abuser's child. How do I start over when I feel stuck?

Answers:

I left with a five-year-old. He has to go to therapy. Their happiness is never worth your life or your babies, and they always get worse.

-J.

You start over by realizing that you have an opportunity to raise a child in a loving home, free from abuse. Let your child be your motivation. You may be sad that your child will grow up without his biological father, but you're really doing your child a favor because you don't want that child to learn abusive behavior by watching you be abused. Change the way you see the situation, and that will help.

-K.

Being a single parent is challenging, but so is raising a child in an abusive home. You don't have to raise your child in that kind of environment. You have options.

-T.

You pick yourself up off the ground and realize you're bringing a new life into this world. Your child needs at least one healthy parent to raise him in a safe and happy environment.

-S.

Most abusers continue to abuse their pregnant partners. It's not safe for you there. You have an obligation to protect your unborn child. It's not just about you anymore.

-G.

Find a safe place for you and your child to go. You don't want to have a miscarriage because of the abuse. It's not an uncommon thing. Abusers don't stop abusing just because you're pregnant.

-I.

At nine months pregnant, my abuser dragged me across the floor by my hair all because I wanted to have sex, and he didn't. If he doesn't care enough not to hurt you, he won't care about the child growing inside of you. Get away.

-S.

The best time to pack up and leave is before the baby comes.

-P.

My abuser told me to get an abortion when he discovered the baby might have Down Syndrome. I don't believe in that because of my faith. I knew I would always choose my child if I had to choose. Today, I have a happy and healthy eleven-year-old with no Down Syndrome.

-K.

It starts in the mind. You must believe you deserve better and will do whatever it takes to get free and raise healthy and happy kids. You may need help for a while, but you can care for your children alone.

-A.

Question:

Has anyone else's child taken the side of the abuser?

Answers:

Yes, my son takes his side. It's heartbreaking because he knows what he's capable of. He witnessed a lot of abuse. He shouldn't be involved.

-M.

Yes. Unfortunately, at times. I don't blame them, though. They're just children.

-U.

No. Mine grew into a beautiful young man and father. I did keep him in counseling. I never told him that his father was horrible, and he always had the choice to talk to his dad. He saw me be strong and walk away. I'm blessed.

-S.

Nope. Mine tells me never to go back to that jerk.

-G.

My two adult sons no longer talk to me because of my abuser. It makes me sad every day.

-B.

Sometimes, you have to realize that if the abuser is their biological dad, a child will always be torn between the two. Try to understand what they're going through. It's not their fault. Kids can't choose their parents.

-Z.

No. They don't speak about him much. I tell them that dad is not a safe person right now and that maybe one day, they can have a relationship with him when they are older. I think they should be able to decide for themselves.

-I.

It happens because they were abused too. Kids always want to please their parents.

-B.

Mine didn't have much respect for him until he passed away. Now it's all lies.

-C.

Section 4:
Staying with an Abuser

"Please know that you can get out and it will not always be an easy road, and it will be lonely at times. But it only gets better, life is too beautiful to live it trapped and abused and hiding under the shame of it all."

-Christine Murray

Question:

Why does my abuser always make me feel like I'm the problem?

Answers:

So they never have to admit their guilt and change. It's a way for them to avoid dealing with their issues.
-K.

Manipulation. They're the real problem.
-C.

Because they like having complete control, and if they admit they're the problem, they will lose that control.
-M.

Because they are cowards, it's the only way they can live with themselves.
-T.

To this day, I still get told that I was the problem, and that's why our relationship didn't work out.
-A.

Because they are immature and insecure, abusers often act macho and puff up, but they're terrified little boys. It's sad how they abuse women to make themselves feel good about themselves.

-B.

Projection to avoid guilt and accountability. Vilifying you makes them believe that the abuse was somehow justified. It is not.

-V.

They do it to break us down. They want us to believe the picture they paint about us instead of who we are. Don't believe the abuser's narrative. Look down deep and see the truth of who you are.

-P.

It's a tactic they use to make us feel crazy and belittle us. I've been there before, and it's hard. I know when it's happening now, but I used to be so weak.

-C.

So he doesn't have to deal with his insecurities and issues.

-O.

Question:

Can an abusive man change?

Answers:

I don't believe they can.

-O.

No, they get worse, a lot worse.

-A.

No. Absolutely not. The change is only temporary.

-B.

Anyone can change if that's what they want to do. Unfortunately, the percentage of abusers who change is slim to none. For a person to change, they have to be willing to admit wrongdoing. Abusers love to blame everyone else for their problems.

-K.

In my experience, yes, if he wants to, but only for someone he has never abused.

-T.

I left him. He moved on and had two children with another woman. It lasted three years; he abused her, too, and almost killed her.
-V.

Anyone can change. Believe actions, not words, because that's the actual proof.
-C.

If they wanted to change, they would have already.
-L.

Question:

Why am I the only woman he's ever hit?

Answers:

Don't believe him. Mine said the same. He even tried to tell me his therapist said he understood since nothing else worked.

-R.

I thought the same thing until I found out more information after digging.

-T.

Me too. I used to beat myself up, wondering what it was about me that made him abuse me until I put the pieces together and realized that his first wife had fled the state with their only son. She didn't do that for no reason.

-K.

I wonder the same thing. I've witnessed him step in and help other women who are being abused, yet he beat me severely. It doesn't make sense. Please don't get stuck on it because nothing abusers do makes sense.

-I.

Abusers are liars. You are probably not the only one he's abused unless you're his first girlfriend. Believe me, it will continue even after you. You just won't know it.
-S.

I wonder the same. At 33 weeks pregnant, my boyfriend pushed me around, got in my face, threatened to break my arm, and punched me in the face.
-C.

Abusers are all about controlling the narrative. They only want you to know the information they give you and believe whatever they say to you. I bet you're not the first and won't be the last.
-H.

I'm sure you're not; they like to lie about that too.
-A.

Question:

Is it normal to feel like I don't know who I am anymore?

Answers:

Stay strong. You are worth it. You have a purpose. Don't ever think less of yourself for a person who's not right in the head.

-A.

What you are feeling is normal. It takes time to find the old you and rebuild the new you. Watch your self-talk and the things you say to yourself. Force yourself to think happy thoughts.

-P.

That's why you must find the strength to leave. He wants you to be so broken that you accept whatever he gives you. You are stronger than you think. You are valuable, but you'll never be able to see it as long as you stay. I know it's easier said than done, but please get out.

-K.

You're experiencing trauma. It's a normal reaction to being abused. Take all your compassion and love for him and give it to yourself.
-A.

It is normal because abusers are very good at belittling you to the point that you feel like nothing. Don't believe the lies. Know that you are worthy and valuable. Your abuser will never be able to see that. You must learn to recognize your own worth.
-C.

Question:

Is Staying Worth It?

Answer:

Only you can decide if it's worth staying in an abusive relationship. By now, I'm sure you've heard the many voices telling you should leave. You already know that. You also already know that you're not living in a healthy environment. I don't know your reasons for wanting to stay or your reasons for wanting to leave, but you have to decide if you're willing to live with the consequences of the choices you're making today.

If you have children with your abuser, are you willing to accept the long-term effects that come with children living in an abusive home? Are you willing to accept that most children who've witnessed abuse go on to have abusive relationships in their adult lives? Are you willing to face the possibility of your children being taken out of your home because your abuser lives with you? These are hard and even unfair questions, but they are real, and real is the only thing that will help you make the right decisions for you and your family.

You must come to the place where you wake up to the reality of your current situation. Is your life in danger?

What would happen to your children if you were no longer here to care for them? Who would take care of them? I know you want your family to work out. I understand you wish your abuser would change and want to wait it out, but what is it costing you? You must make the decisions for your life and be okay with whatever those resulting consequences are, whether good or bad.

I've been where you are. I've felt inadequate and incapable of doing this thing called life alone. I've feared being a single parent and raising children alone. I've also felt the freedom and hope that comes from knowing I have a bright future ahead of me, free from abuse. It all starts with a choice. Choose wisely because your decision will affect not only you but also those that you love.

Section 5:
Leaving an Abuser

"Never forget that walking away from something unhealthy is brave even if you stumble a little on your way out the door."

- Unknown

Question:

How did you find the strength to leave?

Answers:

You don't need strength; you are already strong.

-A.

Joining a support group helped give me the courage to leave, and my local domestic violence counselor.

-N.

By caring about your life and wanting better for yourself.

-J.

You already have it, my dear. You know you are worth more, deserve more, and love yourself more. Things will not improve, but you already know that too.

-L.

You get tired of being unloved and not respected. You can do it. Just leave and don't look back. There are guys who will treat you like a queen.

-M.

When you get tired of waking up every day with someone who says they love you but puts you down every chance they get.
-P.

-You need to set a final boundary, and you'll know when it's time to go.
-H.

I knew I had no other choice, or he would eventually kill me. I had to get myself and my children to a safe place. My biggest regret is not leaving sooner because my son has major PTSD from what he witnessed. It's just not worth it.
-V.

Look inside of yourself; there's a lioness inside of there. It's time to let the world see her.
-R.

One day you'll wake up and realize you don't want to die.
-C.

I realized it when he got mad at me for crying over my dying grandfather. He told me I needed to stay home and not go see him. That's when I knew it was over.
-B.

Enough was enough. I didn't want to keep making excuses for the bruises to my family and friends. I didn't want to keep living a lie.
-H.

Look at what he's done to you and yours, and run!
-L.

I realized that my kid and I deserved better.
-S.

I was back and forth for twenty years because I could see the person I fell in love with. It cost me my life, and that's what I often remind myself of. Get support.
-A.

Question:

How did you stop returning to your abuser after you left?

Answers:

Absolutely no contact. I got a restraining order against him. He cannot contact me, I cannot contact him. I left him one time in twenty-four years for two months. This time was much easier.

-P.

I've been keeping myself busy. Before, I would reach out because I missed him, but last time I got so fed up, I refused to go back. I keep myself busy by getting out of the house and talking to friends and family.

-J.

I literally scream and cry from all of the pain and frustration. I know I can't take the risk of being with him.

-O.

Keep your mind off that person. Remember the trauma and what they did to you.

-A.

You deserve better. Go get your hair done, go to a new city, and meet new people. I try to stay busy.

-T.

I read my bible. I wrote a list of everything I want in a man. My abuser barely fits anything I want. Lol. Somewhere out there, a man is waiting for me to get over a man that doesn't deserve me, so he can fully love me. God has amazing plans, and it doesn't involve being hurt. We just have to trust him.

-A.

Put your phone down and pick up a book.

-S.

Think about how much smarter and more beautiful you are without him.

-T.

Stay distracted; that's the only thing that's ever worked for me. Don't contact him. Don't open the door. Don't respond to emails or text messages.

-P.

My friends promised to remind me of all the bad things he ever did to me because we tend to only remember the good stuff. It worked and made a big difference.

-L.

I text someone I know who will keep me accountable.

-Y.

Keep a journal of everything he did to you. Don't leave anything out. When you start to miss him, read it.

-A.

I took pictures of how I looked after he beat me. Every time I miss him, I remind myself of being in the hospital alone, wanting to die because I didn't want to feel anymore.

-P.

I remind myself that I'm not missing out on anything but being abused and treated like no human should be.

-T.

Question:

When do the nightmares stop?

Answers:

It's been a year, and the nightmares have finally stopped. I still have anxiety, though. Take it slow. You can't heal in one day. One day at a time.

-M.

I've been out nine months. I don't have nightmares every night but more often than not. I realized that it's part of the healing process. It does get better. It just takes time.

-J.

I used to have nightmares a lot in the first couple of years. Looking back, most of it came from fear. He always threatened to kill me, so my dreams would always be of me trying to escape that scenario. One day after looking over my shoulder after taking the garbage out like I always did, God reminded me that he was my protector and didn't want me living in constant fear. After that, the fear slowly faded, and the nightmares eventually stopped.

-K.

Your brain is used to the abuse, so when there's none, you dream. It will go away with time.

-A.

It's trauma. You've been through a lot. Get counseling. You need a safe space to talk about it.

-I.

I once heard that the things you don't deal with show up subconsciously in your dream because your brain needs a way to deal with them. Find a safe person you can talk to. It will get better.

-A.

Question:

How did you stop missing him?

Answers:

Remembering the look in his eyes when he held a gun to my head.

-L.

Thinking about how he never apologized and always felt justified for whatever he did.

-T.

Finding a support system with people who genuinely cared about me. Having people I could tell the whole truth to create accountability so it would be hard to go back.

-M.

Understanding that abuse is like an addiction. It takes time. I got a counselor, and with time and help, I felt free.

-P.

Music! Learning to love my life again. It really helped me through my journey.

-A.

Distract yourself. Keep yourself busy. It helps.

-P.

Remembering the good and bad times we had together. The bad outweighed the good. Right then I knew it wasn't worth it. I learned that freedom and self-worth are more important than any relationship.

-T.

Journaling. Every time I felt down I would write about it and let all my feelings out. It's very therapeutic.

-C.

Every day I get to remember what he did. He put me in a wheelchair. I got a dog to comfort me.

-A.

The fact that I don't have to wake up scared every day. My son and I don't have to walk around on eggshells anymore. I'm happy now.

-T.

I left so many times, the last time I left it didn't hurt and I didn't miss him anymore.

-P.

Never forget what he did to me and how he treated me. I used that as motivation to never go back and to work on myself.

-A.

Question:

How many times did it take you to leave for good?

Answers:

Shoot. Twenty times over eight years if you count overnighters and weekends away.

-B.

Thirty to forty times because he would make love to me so good after he hit me. I finally let go when I started praying and got the strength to start loving myself. I realized one day that if I didn't let go, he would continue hurting me. Plus, I had a daughter who needed me, and I loved her enough to leave. We left the house and everything. I have so much peace now.

-B.

I kicked him out too many times to count. I divorced and remarried him four times because he promised to change. He always knew what to say to get me to take him back and how to break me down, so I thought I couldn't live without him. Looking back, I see how crazy it all was.

-A.

I left eight times and went back. The night was the last time.

-M.

We were together for twenty years. I left eight times. The eighth time I took the kids and got a no contact and protective order. It's been three years. We are healing and learning to live a happy life.

-L.

Three times. The third time was because the police were called and I had to leave. Best thing ever to happen to me.

-S.

It took me three times over a span of five years. Best decision I ever made. He's in prison now for domestic violence against someone else.

-N.

More than ten times probably. It's hard but it's the best thing when you finally do.

-A.

A lot. Finally left after eleven years. It all depends on the person though, when you've had enough.

-P.

I lost count. Been free for ten years though.

-A.

Only once. I tried, but he locked me in the garage and beat me. I fought back and ended up paying for it. A week later my parents came with the cops, and said I was leaving or they would arrest him on his other charges. I didn't want to go because I loved him, but it was the best decision I made. I knew I had to choose between him or my family. I'm very thankful for my loving family.

-M.

More times than I want to admit over the course of nine years.

-P.

I finally learned that I needed to plan it out, not leave spontaneously. I needed to make sure I had money, food, and clothing for the kids; then when I was ready I could go.

-O.

Three. It took me twelve and a half years to leave for good. He's in jail now. I have three children and we couldn't be happier.

-M.

First time. He started in on the dog and our ten-month old baby. I was out. It's amazing what you will put up with but there was no way I was going to allow them to suffer.

-C.

Question:

Has anyone's abuser gone to jail, gotten help, and stopped being abusive towards you?

Answers:

They won't stop. Take care of yourself, because he won't. It will be harder to leave next time. He's on his best behavior now.

-T.

Very, very rare. I've seen it happen once, but that's it.

-P.

No. He went to jail. I got him an attorney and he got out. Less than a year later he tried to kill me and the kids. It only gets worse.

-A.

No. My ex would go to jail and straighten up for three to four months and then go right back to being abusive again.

-L.

Mine went to jail for over a year. Got out doing the same sh--.

-S.

It happened for about two weeks. Then the abuse got worse.

-G.

They're fake, and once they're comfortable with you again, it's back to being mean.

-R.

He went to jail. I recanted, got him out, and brought him home, and it only got worse. He went back to jail, got out again, and got even worse than before. If they want to change they can, but most of these guys would never admit they did anything wrong. They truly believe it's your fault. They think we need to change.

-D.

It's a manipulation tactic they use to make you stay until they get comfortable enough to abuse you again.

L.

Very rare for this to happen. I believe everyone is different, and there are different types of abuse. Do I think some can get help and be successful after? Yes, I do, but those are very rare.

-N.

Oh, God, no! Impossible. Change is only temporary. It always gets worse.

-V.

Jail will only stop them until the fear of legal repercussions diminishes. The honeymoon cycle will start over to win you over again, then your abuser will start to feel spite for you for the fact that he went to jail. He might turn vengeful when the embarrassment and resentment set in over the situation, this time, he will have more fuel for the fire when he turns on you. At least, this is my experience.

-H.

Mine was better for two years straight, then he went right back to it, and it was worse.

-W.

No, in fact, he eventually tried to strangle me to death, raped me, and I had the child.

-H.

What normally happens is they straighten up for a little while, but then the fear of going to jail wears off, and boom! Here comes the abuse again.

-A.

That only happens in fiction, not real life.

-B.

Question:

What was your experience when you went to court to get a protection order?

Answers:

Mine showed up at court and denied everything that happened.
-T.

They tried to serve him. He wouldn't answer the door, so they dropped it.
-R.

I have had one for three years. It was easy because he never showed up to court, but I presented enough evidence.
-S.

Drawn out and kept extending every three months because he kept denying everything. I went to trial and hired a great lawyer with an awesome intern. When the intern played the voicemails of him cursing and threatening me, he got all flustered and admitted to at least choking me. My order was granted instantly.
-V.

I didn't. The cops took all four of them out.
-K.

My abuser's attorney didn't even show up. My attorney and I didn't even have to appear before the judge. He just signed it.
-B.

All of them against him were granted.
-L.

My abuser didn't show up, thank God.
-M.

Question:

How do you end it?

Answers:

On our anniversary, he kidnapped me, assaulted me, and crashed our car into a brick wall. It was the first time I called the cops. They put a two-year no-contact order in place. I filed for legal separation, and he turned it into a divorce. I am so glad to be free.

-K.

Block him. Go no contact even though you miss him. You'll miss him, but you'll learn to live without him. You can do it on your own. Give yourself time to heal.

-J.

The day finally came when I just couldn't continue. It was either leave or lose myself completely. I had to go.

-B.

Stand up for yourself. They hate that. The more you stick up for yourself, the more you believe it, and the faster they run because they realize they've lost control. Does it hurt? Yes. Will you miss him? Yes. Do you want to go down that dark path again? No!

-D.

Listen to the small voice on the inside. Deep down inside, you know he's not good for you.

-E.

You have to decide that you want and deserve better. I know it's easier said than done, but it's your life, and you only get one.

-K.

The cops had to be called because he wouldn't accept that I was done.

-J.

He went to jail, and the court pressed charges against him, so I didn't have to. I miss him, but I would never consider going back.

-M.

Start making a safety plan. Tell yourself that you are done being a victim. Be a victor and leave. Go to the local police station or hospital and ask for services. Someone will be able to assist you from there. Readjust your crown and carry on like the queen you are.

-C.

I always knew it would take something dramatic for me to leave and for us to be over, and that's exactly what happened.

-A.

It's hard. It took me two years to get away in a way where I didn't feel scared.

-B.

Question:

How long does it take to heal before trying to find love again?

Answers:

There's no time limit. Take whatever time you need to feel whole again.

-L.

It takes time to undo the damage and learn to love yourself again. You will get there, though.

-P.

As long as you need. You must understand why you were attracted to your abuser and why you accepted the abuse. I realized that I was codependent and worked through that with a counselor. Also, you must get to the place where you're happy being alone.

-I.

Everyone is different. I thought I was okay after two years, but I was wrong. Don't be afraid to take all the time you need.

-S.

After abuse, I think it's a good idea just to get to know yourself. Sometimes we can want to be with someone so badly that we are willing to sacrifice who we are. Love will always be there. Learn how to love yourself, enjoy yourself, and build yourself up before thinking about getting into another relationship. Get counseling, get good friends, and have a happy career. We need to get to where we're not looking for another person to make us happy and learn to make ourselves happy.

-K.

Ten years. Some women never get to the point where they want to date again. Give yourself time.

-Y.

I think you're ready when you are no longer willing to accept bs from anyone. Get to the place where you are happy to walk away from someone who isn't treating you right. That's when you'll know you're ready.

-M.

I was single for four years. I met a guy a few months ago who seemed like the man of my dreams. It turns out I was wrong. I saw red flags, but I gave him the benefit of the doubt. He almost killed me. Please don't ignore the red flags.

-J.

Listen to your intuition. Don't try to date just because you feel lonely or it's what everyone else is doing. It's your life, and you want the right people in it. That requires a lot of healing, self-reflection, and patience. I know it's not what you probably want to hear, but it will save you a lot of pain and heartache.

-C.

It's been over a year, and I'm still not ready. I don't like it when guys try to flirt with me.

-A.

I enjoy my freedom, so I'm not looking for a relationship. I'm learning to love myself and set boundaries. It's liberating, and I don't feel the need to jump into another relationship.

-D.

I don't know if I could ever trust another person again. I'm going to focus on myself and my children.

-A.

Question:

Why do I miss my abuser?

Answer:

Believe me when I tell you that there is nothing wrong with you for missing the person who abused you. It's very common for victims of domestic violence to miss their abusers. You've spent time with that person, shared your life with them, maybe you were married or had plans to be with them for the rest of your life. Don't allow yourself or others to make you feel stupid for missing someone. What I want you to do is think about your relationship with your abuser. Is it him you miss or the person you wish he would become? That person isn't real. He never was!

Looking back at my abusive relationship, I realize I didn't miss my abuser. How can anyone honestly miss someone who curses, humiliates, degrades, hurts, and constantly criticizes them? Maybe your abuser told you that you couldn't make it without him or that no one would ever want you. Perhaps you miss the attention they gave you or the high you got from the "good" times. None of that was real. It was just a hook o keep you hanging on.

Your abuser only did this to make you believe he cared about you. He didn't. How do I know? People don't abuse people they care about. People cherish and protect the things that are valuable to them. If your abuser cared about you, he would have loved and protected you.

I know the truth hurts, but it's the only thing that will free you. You have to accept that there are just some things you may never understand. You must come to the place where you allow your heart to break so your soul can heal. I know it hurts. I know it's unfair. I know you wish it could be different, but it's not. You've been down that road, knowing it only leads to more pain. You must pick yourself up, brush the dust off, and realize that some people will never know your true worth because they don't even know their own.

I know you want to be his savior. You want to 'love him to life,' but the price is too high. Don't let your love for your abuser cause you to miss the life that God has for you. You will never be happy, satisfied, and live your best life being in a relationship with an abusive person. You must know you deserve better and refuse to accept anything less.

It will initially seem hard and impossible, but I promise it's not. Healing begins when you know your worth and refuse to settle for less than that.

Section 6:
Women of Faith Facing Abuse

You shall know them by their fruits.

- Jesus

Question:

Is abuse God's way of punishing me?

Answer:

In my first marriage, I suffered physical, emotional, and financial abuse at the hand of my husband, who was a professing Christian. Every day I walked on eggshells and lived in terror of the next traumatic event. I was young, and he was older than me, so I trusted his wisdom and judgment. I was wrong. Soon after I got pregnant with my first child, he hit me for the first time. He isolated me from my family and tore me down with his words every chance he got.

He used the Bible to belittle me and make me feel insignificant. After an abusive episode, he refused to apologize and said I had to forgive him because of my faith. He made me believe I was less than him because I was a woman. He further degraded me by making me ask for food. I couldn't do laundry or take our two children outside. I was controlled, dominated, and humiliated.

During those years, I wondered why God had allowed me to suffer. I was a Christian, after all. I wanted to please him and have a happy family. Why did things turn out this way? My answer to all of these questions was that God was punishing me.

Why? I didn't know. He must've loved men more than women, so he allowed my husband to get away with abusing his wife and children. I was angry and bitter. I knew I didn't deserve this, but I couldn't see a way out. My husband controlled all of the finances and told me he would kill me if I ever took his children away from him. I was a prisoner for life, or so I thought.

It's not God's desire for you to be abused. No, he didn't cause it to happen. No, he's not happy about it. He loves you and wants the very best for you. Don't get trapped in a lie as I did by believing that God is punishing you. God is your protector. He will lead and guide you out of abuse. Trust and believe that God is good.

For I know the plans I have for you," declares the LORD, "plans to prosper you and not to harm you, plans to give you hope and a future.
-Jeremiah 21:11

He wants the very best for you. Let him show you how. Read the signs, take the opportunities, and get the resources. Get help and be set free. You are not alone. You are loved.

***Read my story in my book Love Yourself First: How to Heal From Toxic People, Create Healthy Relationships & Become a Confident Woman

Question:

Did your abuser ever use your faith against you?

Answers:

Yes. Mine used to say that if the Bible gave him permission to whip the kids, then he must have permission to whip his wife as well. I left the night he tried to kill me.

-C.

His family said that I must stay and deal with it because divorce wasn't an option. My family who is Catholic has supported me one-hundred percent in leaving and divorcing my abuser. He and his family tried, but God is stronger.

-S.

My abuser said that abusing wives was okay in the Bible.

-T.

Abuse is a sin. Anyone who would try and use your faith against you to make you accept abuse like my ex-husband did is not a Christian, and is not following the example of what they say they believe. God doesn't ask us to submit to sin. If our husband isn't following Christ by his behavior, then we are not to follow him either. I'm glad I understand this now.

-H.

He used the scripture every chance he got to bully me.

-E.

Yes. That was probably the one thing he did multiple times to get me to stay.

-M.

Yes. That's why it's important for you to know what the Bible says for yourself. For a long time, I allowed my pastors to make excuses for my husband's behavior. Instead of protecting me and my children, they protected my abuser. I now know that I have the God-given right to stand up and protect my children. I don't need anyone's permission.

-A.

He would use his religious views to make me think that I didn't deserve to be treated as an equal.

-A.

It took me years to gather everything I needed to leave, but once I did, I never looked back.

-C.

Yeah. The only reason I married my abuser, who was older than me, was because he lied and told me that God said I was his wife. I didn't like him, and I wasn't attracted to him. I was young and naive. I didn't want to disappoint God. I know better now.

-P.

Question:

Was anyone else mad at God for the abuse?

Answers:

No. I think God gave me warning signs. I was just mesmerized by his looks. No. I apologized to God.

-T.

God never sends abusers to us; that's Satan.

-M.

I was angry at God until I understood that God loves me so much that he allowed me to make my own mistakes.

God allows some things in our lives to help us learn lessons. It hurt like hell, but boy, have I learned mine. I will never settle for less again.

-P.

Me. I just had a heated conversation with God. I never wanted any of this. I don't want to be hurt. I didn't want to deal with the aftermath. What did I do wrong? I don't get it.

-D.

I don't blame God because God had nothing to do with it. A lot of people use God's name to do ungodly things. It's up to us to know God for ourselves so that we won't be taken advantage of. God is love, so anyone who doesn't love doesn't know God.

-R.

I used to be like that, but I have forgiven my father and realized that it wasn't anyone's fault but mine.

-L.

Looking back, I can see clear warning signs. I didn't have self-love, ignored my gut instincts, and settled for less than I knew I deserved. That wasn't God's fault. Through all of this, I'm learning to love and value myself. Only then can I teach others to do so.

-I.

Yes, I was so angry because I felt like he had left me. Later, I realized that God was always there watching over me, protecting me, and keeping me through it all.

-U.

Question:

My abuser says he's a Christian

Answer:

What better source to answer this question than the Bible itself? Below is a list of Scriptures that talk about the attributes of a Christian. The Bible says that others will know that we are Christians by our fruit (how we behave and love each other).

You can identify them by their fruit, that is, by the way they act. Can you pick grapes from thorn bushes, or figs from thistles?
-Matthew 7:16

Since we know that Christ is righteous, we also know that all who do what is right are God's children.
-1 John 2:29

A good tree can't produce bad fruit, and a bad tree can't produce good fruit.
-Luke 6:43

Whoever says "I know him" but does not keep his commandments is a liar; and the truth is not in him.
-1 John 2:4

So now I am giving you a new commandment: Love each other. Just as I have loved you, you should love each other.
-John 13:34

By this everyone will know that you are my disciples, if you love one another.
-John 13:35 (NIV)

Such people claim they know God, but they deny him by the way they live. They are detestable and disobedient, worthless for doing anything good.
-Titus 1:16

Dear children, don't let anyone deceive you about this: When people do what is right, it shows that they are righteous, even as Christ is righteous. But when people keep on sinning, it shows that they belong to the devil, who has been sinning since the beginning. But the Son of God came to destroy the works of the devil.
-1 John 3: 7-8

Love means doing what God has commanded us, and he has commanded us to love one another, just as you heard from the beginning.
-2 John 1:6

BE WISE

Having faith doesn't mean being a fool. Be suspicious of anyone who asks you to leave your common sense at the door. God gave you intuition and a brain for a reason, so use it. Never tolerate someone who asks you to violate your self-respect and dignity, no matter who they are or their title. As an abuse survivor, I realized that I allowed abuse to continue because I listened to others I thought were more spiritual than me. I thought listening to them was trusting in God. IT IS NOT!

God wants a personal relationship with you; there is no middleman. You don't need a preacher, teacher, prophet, or anyone else to have a relationship with God for you. God wants you to know him for yourself. He wants to know you personally and hear him for yourself. A relationship with God isn't based on your feelings. You don't have to feel worthy. You have to believe that God loves you. Even if you don't believe it, he will help you if you ask. Try it!

God has given you the ability to protect yourself from abusers and people with ill intentions. You must learn to trust your intuition and learn from your past mistakes. You are capable of making the right choices for yourself. I know it can be hard to trust yourself when you've been trained to doubt and question yourself through abuse. However, it is possible to overcome this and be confident again. Be patient with yourself. Don't stop believing, and don't give up on God.

Question:

Can I divorce my abuser?

Answer:

In a perfect world, you would meet a guy, get married, have children, and live happily ever after. Unfortunately, we don't live in an ideal world. We live in a world where people who are supposed to protect us are sometimes the very ones who hurt us. I know it doesn't make sense. No one gets married thinking that they'll get divorced. I was very torn after experiencing abuse in my first marriage. I stayed for as long as I could. The day came when I was forced to leave because of the abuse. I stayed in a homeless shelter for women, and my abuser found me and tried to kill me.

      I didn't choose abuse; he did. I didn't decide to end my marriage; he did through his consistent abusive behavior. Either way, I believe I had every right to divorce him because he had broken our marriage covenant through being unfaithful, not sexually, but in his behavior. One definition of unfaithful is: disloyal and treacherous. When he held a gun at my head, threatened me with a knife, cursed at me, or hit me, he was being unfaithful. It wasn't God's will for me to be abused. It's not God's will for you to be abused either.

I believe Jesus suffered on the cross so we would no longer have to. God isn't pleased when another person uses force, intimidation, manipulation, and fear to control you. He doesn't even do that. He gives everyone free will. He whom the son sets free is free indeed (John 8:36). God is happy when we love and care for one another. Let us love one another, for love is from God (1 John 4:7). Abuse is the opposite of love. It is evil! What other name is there for a repeated act that harms another person physically, mentally, and emotionally

You don't have to accept abuse from anyone. Whoever tells you differently is LYING and not following the example of Christ. I encourage you to read your Bible. Learn who God is for yourself and get to know who he is and what he has to say about you. In the meantime, read these Scriptures and be encouraged, knowing that God accepts, wants, and loves you.

Scriptures

Husbands, love your wives and never treat them harshly.
-Colossians 3:19

In the same way, you husbands must give honor to your wives. Treat your wife with understanding as you live together. She may be weaker than you are, but she is your equal partner in God's gift of new life. Treat her as you should so your prayers will not be hindered.
-1 Peter 3:7

For husbands, this means love your wives, just as Christ loved the church. He gave up his life for her
-Ephesians 5:25

Dear friends, do not believe everyone who claims to speak by the Spirit. You must test them to see if the spirit they have comes from God. For there are many false prophets in the world.
-1 John 4:1

In the same way, husbands ought to love their wives as they love their own bodies. For a man who loves his wife actually shows love for himself.
-Ephesians 5:28

Submit to one another out of reverence for Christ.
-Ephesians 5:21 (NIV)

Get rid of all bitterness, rage, anger, harsh words, and slander, as well as all types of evil behavior.
-Ephesians 4:31

There is no longer Jew or Gentile, slave or free, male and female. For you are all one in Christ Jesus.
-Galatians 3:28

CONCLUSION

I pray that now you have a clearer understanding of God's will for you. Marriage and relationships are supposed to be mutually loving relationships where both parties seek the best for one another. The man is not greater than the woman, nor is the woman more significant than the man. Both are equal in Christ.

There is neither Jew nor Greek, there is neither bond nor free, there is neither male nor female: for ye are all one in Christ Jesus. **-Galatians 3:8**

No one is perfect, but no one has the right to use God's word against you to manipulate you into submitting to abuse. That is not of God. I pray that you understand that you deserve better. You must choose to give it to yourself. I wish you well. Let God guide you and lead you to the beautiful life he has for you. If your husband professes a change of heart, let his actions be the proof. God doesn't call any of us to be a fool. Use the wisdom he gave you. Be safe and live free.

-With love,
Krystle

ABOUT THE AUTHOR

Krystle Laughter is an international-selling author, certified life coach, mentor, recording artist, and mother of seven. She enjoys writing poetry, spoken word, and music. She is passionate about inspiring others and utilizes her online platforms to empower women through self-love and personal development. A true overcomer and overachiever, Krystle has triumphed to become the woman she is today. Book her as your life coach today if you need help achieving your goals, accountability, motivation, or healing from the past.

Krystle also helps aspiring authors through her author coaching services. She can provide manuscript feedback, create a unique book cover, and develop a beautiful custom layout for your nonfiction book. Please email her at krystlelaughter@gmail.com for inquiries.

Be sure to follow her on YouTube, Instagram, Facebook & Twitter @krystlelaughter for more inspiration.

BOOKS

Love Yourself First

Many women live lives far less than they deserve because they never learned to love themselves. Loving yourself first is the secret to being happy, finding true love, and becoming a confident woman because you teach others how to treat you. If you've ever done love wrong, married or single, this book is for you. In Love Yourself First, you'll learn how to: Heal from the past, teach others to love you by loving yourself, choose relationships that compliment your future, use the "3 A's of Healing", and practice self-love every day.

You're a Diamond!

A 30-Day Devotional for Women

Do you want to start your day off right? Do you need a little encouragement in the morning? If you're looking for a fun, light-hearted way to kickstart your day, You're a Diamond! is perfect. The author shares inspirational stories and heartfelt lessons from her life that will motivate you to go higher and dig deeper. Get the book today!

When I Think of You

Losing a loved one is painful. It's important to remember the good memories you shared. When I Think of You follows a little girl who experiences the joy of remembering a loved one. When I Think of You is the perfect gift for children and adults alike; it provides a sweet way to honor the memory of a lost loved one by meditating on the good times. Share the joy now in...When I Think of You.

Krystle Laughter Academy

AFTER TOXIC
Healing the hurt & breaking the cycle

Write THE BOOK
HOW TO WRITE, STRUCTURE & FINISH YOUR BOOK MANUSCRIPT

SINGLE MOM SCHOOL
From Surviving to Thriving

Practice self-care
Overcome mom guilt
Maintain your identity
Adjust to single parenting
Be the mom your kids need

Many people are stuck because of their past and the things they've experienced. They feel unworthy to receive good things and settle for less in life & relationships. No MORE! Are you ready to discover your worth and learn how to love yourself? At Krystle Laughter Academy, we equip people with tools to help them heal from the past and to become self-published authors. If you want to know more, visit krystlelaughter.org.